THE LITTLE BOOK OF
CHRISTMAS
QUOTES

TRACEY IVELL

This book is sent with
love to

....

....

....

....

....

"Christmas is the day that holds all time together."

Alexander Smith

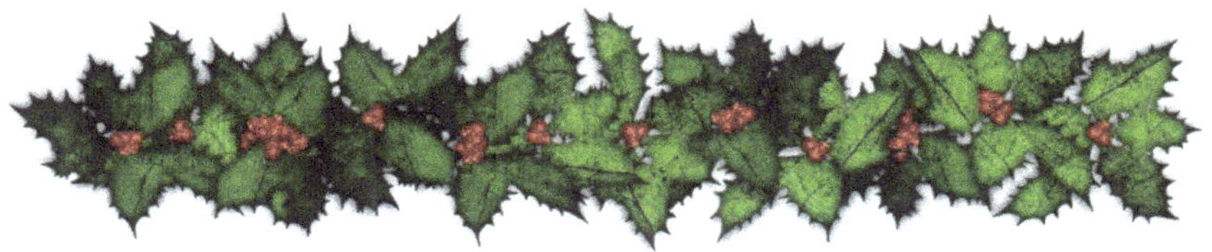

"I have always thought of Christmas time, when it has come round... as a good time; a kind, forgiving, charitable, pleasant time; the only time I know of, in the long calendar of the year, when men and women seem by one consent to open their shut-up hearts freely."

Charles Dickens

"To appreciate the beauty of a snowflake, it is necessary to stand out in the cold"

Aristotle

"The First Noel the Angels did say,
Was to certain poor shepherds in fields as they lay,
In fields where they lay keeping their sheep,
On a cold winter's night that was so deep"

The First Noel, Anonymous (1833)

"I'm dreaming of a white
Christmas but if the white runs
out I'll drink the red"

Anonymous

"And we are better throughout the year for having in spirit, become a child again at Christmas time."

Laura Ingalls Wilder

"Christmas is not as much about opening our presents as opening our hearts."

Janice Maeditere

"In the bleak midwinter frosty wind made moan,
earth stood hard as iron, water like a stone:
snow had fallen, snow on snow, snow on snow,
in the bleak midwinter, long ago."

**In the bleak midwinter
By Christina Georgina Rossetti (c. 1872)**

"May you never be too grown up to search the skies on Christmas Eve."

Anonymous

"Mankind is a great, an immense family. This is proved by what we feel in our hearts at Christmas."

Pope John XXIII

"Snowflakes are kisses

from heaven"

Unknown

"I will honour Christmas in my heart, and try to keep it all the year"

Ebeneezer Scrooge

"Christmas isn't a season. It's a feeling."

Edna Ferber

"Christmas is a season for kindling the fire for hospitality in the hall, the genial flame of charity in the heart."

Washington Irving

"Snowflakes are tiny stars that have fallen from the sky"
Unknown

"Santa Claus is anyone who loves another and seeks to make them happy; who gives himself by thought or word or deed in every gift that he bestows."

Edwin Osgood Grover

"T'was the night before Christmas, when all through the house, not a creature was stirring, not even a mouse."

Clement Clarke Moore

"Be naughty –

save Santa the trip"

Unknown

"O Christmas Tree, O Christmas Tree... How lovely are your branches"

Ernst Anschutz

"O Tannenbaum, o Tannenbaum, Wie treu sind deine Blätter!"

"Where we love is home - home that our feet may leave, but not our hearts"

Oliver Wendell Holmes

"When your room sparkles with the lights on the Christmas Tree, life just seems to sparkle a little more too"

Unknown

"The rooms were very still while the pages were softly turned and the winter sunshine crept in to touch the bright heads and serious faces with a Christmas greeting"

Louisa May Alcott

"God bless us, everyone"

Tiny Tim, Scrooge
Charles Dickens

"Christmas is the season when
you buy this year's gifts
with next year's money"

Unknown

"Christmas is not a time nor a season, but a state of mind."

Calvin Collidge

"May your Christmas be furry and bright

Happy Paw-lidays!"

Unknown

"Silent night, Holy night
All is calm, all is bright
Round yon Virgin, mother and
child
Holy infant, so tender and mild,
Sleep in heavenly peace,
Sleep in heavenly peace"

Silent Night, Joseph Mohr 1818

"Heap on the wood!
- the wind is chill;
But let it whistle as it will,
We'll keep our Christmas
merry still."

Sir Walter Scott

"For to us a child is born, to us a son is given, and the government will be on his shoulders. And he will be called Wonderful Counselor, Mighty God, Everlasting Father, Prince of Peace"

Isaiah 9:6

"I heard the bells on Christmas Day
There old familiar carols play
And wild and sweet, the words
repeat
Of peace on earth, good-will to
men."

Henry Wadsworth Longfellow

"For it is in giving that we receive."

Francis of Assisi

"We three kings of Orient are;
Bearing gifts we traverse afar,
Field and fountain, moor and mountain,
Following yonder star."

John H. Hopkins 1857

"Christmas is the day that holds all time together."

Alexander Smith

"Perhaps the best Yuletide decoration is being wreathed in smiles."

Anonymous

But the angel said to them, "Do not be afraid. I bring you good news that will cause great joy for all the people."

Luke 2:10

The light of the Christmas star to you,
The warmth of home and hearth to you,
The cheer and good will of friends to you,
The joy of a thousand angels to you,
The love of the Son,
And God's peace to you.

Irish Christmas Blessing

O Come, all ye faithful, joyful and triumphant!
O come ye, O come ye, to Bethlehem
Come and behold him
Born the King of Angels
O Come, let us adore him
O Come, let us adore him
O Come, let us adore him
Christ the Lord

John Francis Wade 1751

"Snow brings out the child in all of us."

Unknown

"I don't know what to do!" cried Scrooge, laughing and crying in the same breath; and making a perfect Laocoön of himself with his stockings. "I am as light as a feather, I am as happy as an angel, I am as merry as a school-boy. I am as giddy as a drunken man"

Ebeneezer Scrooge

"Christmas dinner is when we all eat far too much turkey, drink a little too much wine, indulge in pudding and chocolates and then fall fast asleep in front of a roaring fire!"

Unknown

"This is quite the season indeed for friendly meetings. At Christmas everybody invites their friends about them, and people think little of even the worst weather. I was snowed up at a friend's house once for a week. Nothing could be pleasanter."

Jane Austen, Emma

O little town of Bethlehem, how still
we see thee lie!
Above thy deep and dreamless
sleep, the silent starts go by.
Yet in thy dark streets shineth, the
everlasting light;
The hopes and fears of all the years
are met in thee tonight.

Phillips Brooks 1868

At Christmas play and make good cheer, for Christmas comes but once a year.

Thomas Tusser

"It's not what's under the Christmas tree that matters, it's who is around it."

Anonymous

"The holly and the ivy

When they are both full grown,

Of all the trees that are in the wood

The holly bears the crown."

1871

"The magic of Christmas is in the little things, like the first sip of hot cocoa on a cold night, the sound of children's laughter, and the warmth of a loved one's embrace"

Unknown

And there were shepherds living out in the fields nearby, keeping watch over their flocks at night. An angel of the Lord appeared to them, and the glory of the Lord shone around them, and they were terrified.

Luke 2:8-9

Here we come a-wassailing
Among the leaves so green;
Here we come a-wand'ring
So fair to be seen.

Love and joy come to you,
And to you your wassail too;
And God bless you and send you a
Happy New Year
And God send you a Happy New Year.

1850

"Christmas is a season for giving, but the greatest gift we can give is our time and presence."

Unknown

Snowflakes are nature's way of showing that even the smallest things can be beautiful and intricate."

Unknown

"The best Christmas ornaments are those bought with love ....which bring memories year after year"

Unknown

"Christmas is a time to believe in the impossible, to hope for the best, and to love unconditionally."

Unknown

Hark! The herald angels sing,
Glory to the new born King:
Peace on earth, and mercy mild,
God and sinners reconciled.
Joyful, all ye nations, rise
Join the triumph of the skies;
With th'angelic hosts proclaim,
"Christ is born in Bethlehem"

1840

"May the Christmas spirit inspire you to be kind, compassionate, and generous to others"

Unknown

"The taste of Christmas dinner is the taste of home, the taste of family, and the taste of love."

Unknown

"The smell of a real Christmas tree is the essence of the holiday season."

Unknown

"Santa Claus is a symbol of hope and magic, a reminder that anything is possible if you believe."

Unknown

"The holiday season is a time to come together as a community and to celebrate the wonderful diversity of our cultures."

Unknown

"Dashing through the snow
On a one horse open sleigh
O'er the fields we go,
Laughing all the way
Bells on bob tail ring,
making spirits bright
What fun it is to laugh and sing
A sleighing song tonight"

Jingle Bells

James Lord Pierpont 1857

"The table is set, the food is cooking, and the house is filled with the smell of Christmas dinner. It's the most wonderful time of the year!"

Unknown

"At this beautiful time of year it is important to reflect on our blessings and give back to those in need."

Unknown

"There is nothing in the world so irresistibly contagious as laughter and good humour"

Charles Dickens

Should old acquaintance be forgot,
and never brought to mind?
Should auld acquaintance be forgot,
and auld lang syne?
For auld lang syne, my jo,
For auld lang syne
We'll tak' a cup o' kindness yet,
For auld lang syne.

Robert Burns 1788

"May the joy of Christmas fill your home and heart, and may the spirit of the season stay with you all year long"

Unknown

"A Christmas tree is a symbol of the Christmas spirit, a reminder of the love and giving that makes the holiday season so special."

Unknown

"May your celebrations be filled with all the things you love: delicious food, good company, and the warmth of the holiday spirit."

Unknown

"We are at that very special time of year when it is a time to create new memories and to cherish the old ones."

Unknown

A merry Christmas to everybody! A happy New Year to all the world!"

Ebeneezer Scrooge
A Christmas Carol

Charles Dickens

Merry
Christmas
And a
Happy
New
Year

74